YOU'RE THE CHEF

# SLURPABLE Smoothies AND Drinks

Kari Cornell   Photographs by **Brie Cohen**

M MILLBROOK PRESS • MINNEAPOLIS

For my mom, who taught me how to experiment in the kitchen; and for Will, Theo, and Brian, who cheerfully sampled every smoothie and drink I put on the table —K.C.

For Morgon Mae Schultz —B.C.

Photography by Brie Cohen
Food in photographs prepared by chef David Vlach
Illustrations by Laura Westlund/Independent Picture Service
The image on page 5 is used with the permission of © iStockphoto.com/stuartbur.

Allergy alert: The recipes in this book contain ingredients to which some people can be allergic. Anyone with food allergies or sensitivities should follow the advice of a physician or other medical professional.

Millbrook Press
A division of Lerner Publishing Group, Inc.
241 First Avenue North
Minneapolis, MN 55401 U.S.A.

Website address: www.lernerbooks.com

Main body text set in Felbridge Std Regular 11/14.
Typeface provided by Monotype Typography.

Library of Congress Cataloging-in-Publication Data

Cornell, Kari A.
Slurpable smoothies and drinks /
by Kari Cornell ; photographs by Brie Cohen.
pages   cm. — (You're the chef)
Includes index.
ISBN 978-0-7613-6639-3 (library binding : alkaline paper)
ISBN 978-1-4677-1715-1 (eBook)
1. Smoothies (Beverages)—Juvenile literature.  2. Beverages—Juvenile literature.  I. Title.
TX815.C57 2014
641.87'5—dc23                                                                    2012048904

Manufactured in the United States of America
1 – CG – 7/15/13

# TABLE OF CONTENTS

Are you ready to make some slurpalicious drinks and smoothies? YOU can be the chef and make food for yourself and your family. These easy recipes are perfect for a chef who is just learning to cook. And they're so delicious, you'll want to make them again and again!

I developed these recipes with the help of my kids, who are six and eight years old. They can't do all the cooking on their own yet, but they can do a lot.

Can't get enough of cooking? Check out www.lerneresource.com for bonus recipes, healthful eating tips, links to cooking technique videos, and more!

# BEFORE YOU START

**Reserve your space!** Always ask for permission to work in the kitchen.

**Find a helper!** You will need an adult helper for some tasks. Talk with this person to decide what steps you can do on your own and what steps the adult will help with.

**Make a plan!** Read through the whole recipe before you start cooking. Do you have the ingredients you'll need? If you don't know what a certain ingredient is, see page 31 to find out more. Do you understand each step? If you don't understand a technique, such as *chill* or *slice*, turn to page 7. At the beginning of each recipe, you'll see how much time you'll need to prepare the recipe and to cook it. The recipe will also tell you how many servings it makes. Small drawings at the top of each recipe let you know what major kitchen equipment you'll need—such as a stovetop, a blender, or a microwave.

stovetop

blender

knives

microwave

oven

**Wash up!** Always wash your hands with soap and water before you start cooking. And wash them again after you touch raw eggs, meat, or fish.

**Get it together!** Find the tools you'll use, such as measuring cups or a mixing bowl. Gather all the ingredients you'll need. That way you won't have to stop to look for things once you start cooking.

# SAFETY TIPS

**That's sharp!** Your adult helper needs to be in the kitchen when you are using a knife, a grater, or a peeler. If you are doing the cutting, use a cutting board. Cut away from your body, and keep your fingers away from the blade.

**That's hot!** Be sure an adult is in the kitchen if you use the stove or the oven. Your adult helper can help you cook on the stove and take hot things out of the oven.

**Tie it back!** If you have long hair, tie it back or wear a hat. If you have long sleeves, roll them up. You want to keep your hair and clothing out of the food and away from flames or other heat sources.

**Turn that handle!** When cooking on the stove, turn the pot handle toward the back. That way, no one will accidentally bump the pot and knock it off the stove.

**Wash it!** If you are working with raw eggs or meat, you need to keep things extra clean. After cutting raw meat or fish, wash the knife and the cutting board right away. They must be clean before you use them to cut anything else.

**Go slowly!** Take your time when you're working. When you are doing something for the first time, such as peeling or grating, be sure not to rush.

## Above all, have fun!

### Finish the job right!

One of your most important jobs as a chef is to clean up when you're done. Wash the dishes with soap and warm water. Wipe off the countertop or the table. Put away any unused ingredients. The adults in your house will be more excited for you to cook next time if you take charge of cleaning up.

# COOKING TOOLS

bowls

can opener

cheesecloth

cookie sheet

cutting board

dry measuring cups

fork

ice-cream scoop

knives

ladle

liquid measuring cup

loose tea ball

measuring spoons

pitcher

plastic container

saucepans

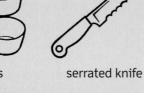
serrated knife

slotted spoon

spoon

vegetable peeler

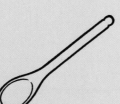
whisk

wooden spoon

# TECHNIQUES

**blend:** to stir together with a spoon, whisk, or blender until well mixed

**boil:** to heat liquid on a stovetop until it starts to bubble

**chill:** to place a food in the refrigerator to make it cold

**chop:** to cut food into small pieces using a knife

**cover:** to put a lid on a pan or pot containing food

**discard:** to throw away or put in a compost bin. Discarded parts of fruits and vegetables and eggshells can be put in a compost bin, if you have one.

**garnish:** to decorate a finished food or drink before serving

**mix:** to stir food using a spoon or fork

**serrated:** a tool, such as a knife, that has a bumpy edge

**set aside:** to put nearby in a bowl or plate or on a clean workspace

**score:** to lightly cut the surface of a food with a knife, taking care not to slice through to the other side

**slice:** to cut food into thin pieces

## MEASURING

To measure **dry ingredients**, such as sugar or flour, spoon the ingredient into a measuring cup until it is full. Then use the back of a table knife to level it off. Do not pack it down unless the recipe tells you to. Do not use measuring cups made for liquids.

When you're measuring a **liquid**, such as milk or water, use a clear glass or plastic measuring cup. Set the cup on the table or a counter and pour the liquid into the cup. Pour slowly and stop when the liquid has reached the correct line.

Don't measure your ingredients over the bowl they will go into. If you accidentally spill, you might have way too much!

serves 4

preparation time: 15 minutes
freezing time: 2 hours or overnight

## ingredients:

1 medium banana
2 cups fresh strawberries
  (1 16-ounce package)
1 large ripe mango
1½ cups orange juice
½ cup strawberry or banana
  yogurt
¼ teaspoon ground cardamom
  (optional)

## equipment:

knife
cutting board
2-cup plastic container with
  tight-fitting lid
paper towels
blender
serrated knife
liquid measuring cup
½-cup measuring cup
measuring spoons
4 juice glasses
4 straws

### TRY THIS!

If fresh mango isn't available, you can use **frozen mango** or other **fresh fruits,** such as **peaches, raspberries, kiwis,** or additional **strawberries.**

# Mango Fandango Smoothie

This quick and easy drink is a tasty and nutritious way to start the day. If you prepare the ingredients the night before, you can even make it on a school day.

1. **Peel** the banana and discard the peel. Use a cutting board and a knife to **slice** the banana into ¼-inch-thick rounds. If you want your smoothie nice and thick, **freeze** the banana slices. Place the slices into a plastic container with a tight-fitting lid. Put the container in the freezer for a couple of hours or overnight. (If you're short on time, you can skip the freezing step.)

2. **Wash** the strawberries and the mango in cool water. Pat dry with paper towels.

3. Use the cutting board and the knife to carefully **cut** around the strawberry stems. Discard the stems, and add the strawberries to a blender.

4. Ask an adult to help you cut the mango. On the cutting board, balance the mango on the ridge that runs lengthwise along the fruit. Use a serrated knife to **slice** away the fruit on both sides of the hard pit inside the fruit. Discard the pit. Place the first half skin side down on the cutting board. **Score** the flesh into ¼-inch squares, creating a checkerboard pattern. Reach one hand underneath the skin, and press it up to turn the half "inside out." Carefully slide the knife between the fruit and the skin. Then **cut** each square of the checkerboard from the skin. Repeat with the second half. Add the mango pieces to the blender.

5. **Add** the frozen banana slices, orange juice, and yogurt to the blender. **Add** the cardamom, if desired.

6. Put the lid on the blender, and **blend** on high until the smoothie is well mixed. If the mixture is too thick, unplug the blender, remove the lid, and use a spoon to stir the solid ingredients away from the blender blade. NEVER put your hand into a blender. You may also add more orange juice to thin the mixture.

7. **Pour** the smoothie into 4 juice glasses, and serve each with a straw.

serves 4

preparation time: 15 minutes
freezing time: 2 hours or overnight

### ingredients:

2 medium bananas
1 cup fresh spinach or other
    mild greens
1 cucumber
20 fresh mint leaves
6 sprigs parsley
1½ cups limeade

### equipment:

knife
cutting board
2-cup plastic container with
    tight-fitting lid
measuring cups—1 cup, ½ cup
paper towels
vegetable peeler
blender
4 juice glasses
4 straws

# Green Power Smoothie

Don't let the color of this tasty drink fool you.
It's sweet and refreshing—and it's a great way
to get some of your daily veggies!

1. **Peel** one banana and discard the banana peel. Use a cutting board and a knife to slice the banana into ¼-inch-thick rounds. Repeat with the other banana. If you want your smoothie nice and thick, **freeze** the banana slices. Place the slices into a plastic container with a tight-fitting lid. Put the container in the freezer for a couple of hours or overnight. (If you're short on time, you can skip the freezing step.)

2. Measure 1 cup spinach leaves. Then **wash** the spinach leaves, the cucumber, the mint leaves, and the parsley in cool water. Pat dry with paper towels.

3. Use a knife and a cutting board to cut the cucumber in half. Wrap one half in plastic wrap to save for another time. Use the vegetable peeler to **peel** the skin from the other half. Discard the peels. Use the knife to **slice** the peeled cucumber into ¼-inch-thick rounds. Cut enough to measure ½ cup.

4. **Add** the sliced cucumber and the mint leaves to the blender.

5. **Remove** enough leaves from the parsley stems to fill ¼ cup. **Add** the parsley to the blender.

6. **Add** the frozen banana slices, the limeade, and the spinach leaves to the blender. Put the lid on the blender, and **blend** on high until the smoothie is well mixed. If the mixture is too thick, unplug the blender, remove the lid, and use a spoon to stir the solid ingredients away from the blender blade. NEVER put your hand into a blender. You may also add more limeade to thin the mixture.

7. **Pour** into 4 juice glasses and serve each with a straw.

## TRY THIS!

Mix and match the ingredients of this smoothie to find a flavor you really like. If you don't like or can't find fresh mint, don't add mint leaves. Try **kiwi** instead of the cucumber. Or replace the spinach with **Swiss chard**. Experiment! But be sure to replace the ingredient you've taken out with the same amount of the new ingredient.

Try using **lemonade** or **apple juice** instead of limeade.

serves 4

refrigeration time: 1 to 2 hours
preparation time: 20 minutes
freezing time: 2 hours or overnight

## ingredients:

1 14-ounce can light coconut
  milk, chilled
1 14-ounce can pineapple
  chunks in juice, chilled
2 ripe bananas
5 kiwis

## equipment:

knife
cutting board
2–cup plastic container with
  tight-fitting lid
paper towels
vegetable peeler
blender
can opener
4 juice glasses
4 straws

**TRY THIS!**
If you're not crazy about kiwis, leave them out and use another 14-ounce can of pineapple instead. Before adding, drain the juice.

# Kiddie Kiwi Colada

This drink mixes the tropical flavors of coconut, pineapple, bananas, and kiwi. Perfect on a hot, summer afternoon—or anytime!

1. **Chill** the cans of coconut milk and pineapple in the refrigerator for 1 to 2 hours.

2. **Peel** a banana and discard the banana peel. Use a cutting board and a knife to **slice** the banana into ¼-inch-thick rounds. Repeat with the other banana. If you want your smoothie nice and thick, **freeze** the banana slices. Place the slices into a plastic container with a tight-fitting lid. Put the container in the freezer for a couple of hours or overnight. (If you're short on time, you can skip the freezing step.)

3. **Wash** the kiwis in cool water and pat dry with paper towels.

4. On the cutting board, **cut** off the top and bottom of one kiwi. Use a sharp vegetable peeler to **remove** the skin. Start at the top of the fruit and carefully peel down toward the bottom. Repeat this all the way around the fruit. (If the kiwi is very soft, have an adult peel it with a knife.) Then use a knife to **slice** the kiwi into round slices ¼-inch thick. Repeat with the other kiwis. Set aside four slices. Put the rest in a blender.

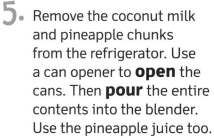

5. Remove the coconut milk and pineapple chunks from the refrigerator. Use a can opener to **open** the cans. Then **pour** the entire contents into the blender. Use the pineapple juice too.

6. **Add** the frozen bananas to the blender. Cover the blender with the lid, and **blend** until smooth and creamy. **Pour** into 4 juice glasses. **Garnish** each glass with a kiwi slice and serve with straws.

serves 4

preparation time: 10 minutes

**ingredients:**
2 cups vanilla ice cream
½ cup grape juice
¼ cup milk

**equipment:**
ice-cream scoop
liquid measuring cup
blender
4 juice glasses
4 straws

# Purple Cow Shake

This tangy mix of grape juice and vanilla ice cream makes for a tasty, drinkable dessert.

1. Use a liquid measuring cup to **measure** the ice cream. **Add** it to a blender.

2. **Add** grape juice and milk.

3. Put the lid on the blender, and **blend** until smooth and creamy.

4. **Pour** into 4 juice glasses, add straws, and serve.

## TRY THIS!

Make this shake with your favorite juices. Orange juice will give you a Creamsicle flavor. Apricot or mango **nectar** is delicious too.

For a lighter version of this shake, use vanilla frozen yogurt.

# Turkish-Style Yogurt Drink

Ever think about drinking your yogurt instead of eating it with a spoon? In Turkey, kids drink their yogurt all the time. It's called *ayran*. If you're a fan of plain yogurt, give this recipe a try.

1. In a blender, **combine** plain yogurt, half and half, cold water, ice cubes, and salt.

2. Put the lid on the blender, and **blend** until the mixture is well-combined and frothy. Enjoy over ice cubes.

serves 3 to 4

preparation time: 5 minutes

**ingredients:**
1½ cups plain, lowfat yogurt
¼ cup half and half
1 cup cold water
2 ice cubes
¼ teaspoon salt

**equipment:**
measuring cups—½ cup,
   ¼ cup
liquid measuring cup
measuring spoons
blender

## TRY THIS!

For more flavor, add 5 mint leaves and ¼ cup peeled, chopped **cucumber** in step 1.

You can also make a sweet version of this drink with your favorite **fruit-flavored yogurt**. Leave out the salt.

serves 4

refrigeration time: 2 hours
preparation time: 10 minutes

## ingredients:

1 cup pineapple juice, chilled
1 8-ounce jar maraschino cherries
   with juice, chilled
2 cups sparkling apple
   juice, chilled
3 oranges
2 limes
2 lemons
8 ice cubes

## equipment:

paper towels
serrated knife
cutting board
medium bowl
spoon
2-quart pitcher
wooden spoon
4 juice glasses

# Cherry Fizz Punch

Serve this colorful, festive punch at a summer party.
Your friends and family will love it!

1. **Chill** the pineapple juice, the maraschino cherries, and the sparkling apple juice in the refrigerator for at least 2 hours. (Longer is fine.)

2. **Wash** the oranges, the limes, and the lemons with warm water and pat dry with paper towels.

3. Use a serrated knife and a cutting board to **cut** 1 orange into ¼-inch-thick rounds. Set the slices aside.

4. On the cutting board, **cut** another orange in half. **Squeeze** one half into a medium bowl to get the juice out. You will need to **scoop** out the seeds with a small spoon. Then squeeze the juice from the other half. Repeat with the other 2 oranges. **Pour** the orange juice into a 2-quart pitcher.

5. **Repeat** step 4 with the limes and the lemons, using the same bowl.

6. **Pour** the pineapple juice, the sparkling apple juice, and the maraschino cherries and all their juice into the pitcher. **Stir** with a wooden spoon to mix the punch.

7. **Add** 2 ice cubes to each of 4 juice glasses. **Pour** the punch into the glasses. **Garnish** each glass with an orange slice and serve.

## TRY THIS!

Any combination of citrus fruits tastes great in this recipe. If sweet pink grapefruit, blood oranges, or key limes are available, try those. (You'll need about 3 key limes to equal the juice of 1 regular lime.)

Try substituting a canned juice spritzer for the 2 cups of sparkling apple juice. A mango or cherry spritzer is super tasty in this recipe too.

serves 4

preparation time: 35 minutes

## ingredients:

1 16-ounce package fresh
   strawberries
¼ cup sugar
½ teaspoon vanilla extract
7 or 8 lemons
⅓ cup honey
2 cups cold water
12 ice cubes

## equipment:

paper towels
knife
cutting board
small mixing bowl
measuring cups—1 cup, ⅓ cup,
   ¼ cup
measuring spoons
wooden spoon
small bowl
spoon
liquid measuring cup
blender
4 juice glasses

# Strawberry Lemonade

This lemonade tastes like summertime in a glass. Yum!

1. **Wash** the strawberries in cool water and pat dry with paper towels.

2. Use a cutting board and a knife to cut around the stem of a strawberry. Discard the stem. Then **cut** the strawberry into thin slices. Repeat with the other strawberries. Cut enough to measure 2 cups. **Place** the strawberry slices into a small mixing bowl.

3. **Add** sugar and vanilla extract to the strawberry slices. **Stir** with a wooden spoon until well mixed. Allow the strawberries to sit for 30 minutes.

4. While the strawberries sit, **wash** the lemons in warm water and pat dry with paper towels.

5. Use the knife and the cutting board to slice one lemon into ¼-inch-thick rounds. Set aside.

6. **Cut** another lemon in half. **Squeeze** one half into a small bowl to get the juice out. You will need to **scoop** out the seeds with a small spoon. Then squeeze the juice from the other half. Repeat with the other lemons, until you have ½ cup of juice.

7. When the strawberries are done sitting, **pour** them and their juice into the blender. Put the lid on the blender, and **blend** until smooth.

8. **Add** the lemon juice, honey, cold water, and 4 ice cubes to the blender. Put the lid on the blender and **blend** thoroughly.

9. **Add** two ice cubes each to 4 juice glasses, and **pour** lemonade into the glasses. **Garnish** the top of each glass with a lemon slice and serve.

serves 4

preparation time: 10 minutes

## ingredients:

1 cup orange juice, chilled
1 cup cranberry juice, chilled
1 orange
2 tablespoons honey
1 cup plain sparkling water
8 ice cubes

## equipment:

paper towel
serrated knife
cutting board
2-quart pitcher
liquid measuring cup
tablespoon
wooden spoon
4 8-ounce glasses

# Cranberry-Orange Spritzer

This tangy-sweet drink tastes great in the summer or in the fall. Try mixing and matching your favorite juice combinations.

**1.** If the orange and cranberry juices are not cold, **place** them in the refrigerator to chill.

**2.** **Wash** the orange in warm water. Rinse thoroughly and pat dry with a paper towel.

**3.** Use a serrated knife and a cutting board to **slice** the orange into ¼-inch-thick rounds. Set the slices aside.

4. In a 2-quart pitcher, **add** cranberry juice, orange juice, and honey. Use a wooden spoon to **stir** the mixture.

5. **Place** 2 ice cubes in each of 4 glasses. **Pour** ½ cup of the cranberry-orange juice mixture in each glass.

6. **Add** ¼ cup sparkling water to each glass. **Garnish** with an orange slice. Serve immediately.

## TRY THIS!

For a lemony treat, use **lemonade** in place of the orange juice. Garnish with **lemon slices**.

Use any favorite **red juice** instead of the plain cranberry juice. **Pomegranate, cherry,** or **cran-raspberry** are all delicious.

serves 6

preparation time: 10 minutes
freezing time: 2 to 3 hours

## ingredients:

1 16-ounce package fresh
   strawberries
¼ cup strawberry yogurt (or one
   yogurt tube)
1 tablespoon honey
1 can frozen orange juice
   concentrate

## equipment:

paper towels
knife
cutting board
measuring cup—¼ cup
measuring spoons
blender
2-quart pitcher
wooden spoon
liquid measuring cup
cookie sheet
6 3-ounce paper or plastic cups
6 craft sticks or plastic spoons
small bowl
ziplock freezer bag

# Strawberry Yogurt Pops

Nothing's better on a hot summer day than a cold,
refreshing Popsicle. Think of it as a smoothie on a stick!
Be sure to make these treats ahead of time, as
they will need a couple of hours to freeze.

**1.** **Wash** strawberries in cool water and pat dry
with paper towels.

**2.** Use a cutting board and a
knife to carefully **cut** around
the strawberry stems. Discard
the stems, and **add** the
strawberries to the blender.

**3.** **Add** strawberry yogurt and honey to the blender.

**4.** **Open** the can of orange juice concentrate. **Add** 1
tablespoon of the frozen concentrate to the blender.

5. In a pitcher, **make** the rest of the orange juice according to the instructions on the can.

6. **Add** ⅓ cup of the orange juice to the blender. Put the rest of the orange juice in the refrigerator to drink later. **Blend** the mixture in the blender until smooth.

*Turn the page for more Strawberry Yogurt Pops*

## TRY THIS!

To make a banana pop, replace strawberries with 2 sliced **bananas**, replace strawberry yogurt with **banana yogurt**, and use **pineapple juice** instead of orange juice.

To make a raspberry pop, use **raspberries, raspberry yogurt, cranberry juice,** and **orange juice concentrate.**

To make a tropical pop, replace strawberries with 1 14-ounce can **pineapple chunks** and 1 peeled and sliced **kiwi.** Replace strawberry yogurt with **pineapple yogurt.**

*Strawberry Yogurt Pops continued*

7. **Place** 6 3-ounce cups right side up on a cookie sheet. **Pour** the thick strawberry mixture evenly into the cups.

8. **Place** a craft stick or a spoon into the center of each cup.

9. **Place** the pan on a flat surface in the freezer. **Freeze** for 2 hours, or until the pops are firm.

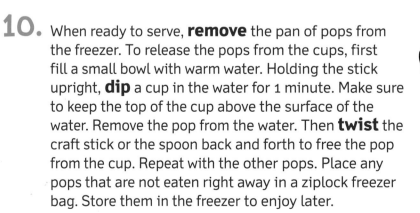

10. When ready to serve, **remove** the pan of pops from the freezer. To release the pops from the cups, first fill a small bowl with warm water. Holding the stick upright, **dip** a cup in the water for 1 minute. Make sure to keep the top of the cup above the surface of the water. Remove the pop from the water. Then **twist** the craft stick or the spoon back and forth to free the pop from the cup. Repeat with the other pops. Place any pops that are not eaten right away in a ziplock freezer bag. Store them in the freezer to enjoy later.

# Sweet Soda Float

This popular root beer float has been around for ages. Here's a chance to try out other favorite soda flavors.

serves 4

preparation time: 5 minutes

**ingredients:**
2 cups vanilla ice cream or frozen yogurt
24 ounces (3 cups) orange soda, cherry soda, ginger ale, or root beer

**equipment:**
ice-cream scoop
4 glasses
liquid measuring cup
4 straws

1. **Scoop** 2 scoops of ice cream or frozen yogurt into each of 4 glasses.

2. **Pour** ¾ cup soda into each glass.

3. **Add** straws and serve.

## TRY THIS!
Mix and match flavors of ice cream and soda to create your own custom float. Try **chocolate ice cream** with **cream soda, strawberry ice cream** with **ginger ale,** or **cherry ice cream** with **cherry soda.**

# Hot Apple Cider

Mmmm, nothing tastes better on a cool, fall day than a steaming cup of spiced hot apple cider. Be sure to let the drink cool slightly before trying it, so you don't burn your tongue!

serves 4 to 6

preparation time: 5 to 10 minutes
cooking time: 30 minutes

## ingredients:

2½ cups apple cider
1 cup cranberry juice
1 cup orange juice
1 tablespoon sugar
1 teaspoon whole allspice
1 teaspoon whole cloves
2 cinnamon sticks

## equipment:

liquid measuring cup
measuring spoons
medium saucepan
small piece cheesecloth or
   loose tea ball
slotted spoon
ladle
4 to 6 mugs

1. In a medium saucepan, **add** apple cider, cranberry juice, orange juice, and sugar.

2. If you are using a loose tea ball, **fill** it with allspice and whole cloves. Then skip to step 4.

3. If you are using cheesecloth, **cut** a 5-inch square from a piece of cheesecloth. In the center of the square, **place** the allspice, whole cloves, and 2 cinnamon sticks. Using your right hand, pick up the top right corner of the cheesecloth. With your left hand, pick up the bottom left corner of the cloth. Pull these two corners together over the top of the spices. **Tie** the ends into a tight double knot. Do the same with the top left corner and the bottom right corners, tying tightly to secure the loose spices.

4. **Place** the cheesecloth or the loose tea ball into the cider mixture in the saucepan. If you are using the tea ball, place the two cinnamon sticks into the mixture separately.

5. Turn the burner under the saucepan on medium. **Heat** the cider mixture until warmed through and well spiced, about 30 minutes.

6. **Remove** spices and cinnamon sticks with a slotted spoon. Use a ladle to scoop the hot cider into mugs.

## TRY THIS!

For a sweeter cider, substitute **cherry** or **cran-raspberry juice** for the cranberry juice.

If you like **honey**, use an equal amount in place of the sugar.

Leftover hot cider can be stored in a jar in the refrigerator. The spiced drink is just as good over ice on warmer autumn days.

Serves 4

preparation time: 15 minutes
cooking time: 8 to 10 minutes

## ingredients:

2½ cups whole milk
2 cinnamon sticks
4 ounces semisweet baking
  chocolate
¼ cup semisweet chocolate
  chips
1 tablespoon sugar
1 teaspoon vanilla extract
1 cup mini marshmallows

## equipment:

liquid measuring cup
medium saucepan
slotted spoon
measuring cups—1 cup, ¼ cup
measuring spoons
wooden spoon
whisk
4 mugs

# Homemade Hot Chocolate

Real hot chocolate is easy to make, and it's so tasty.

1. **Pour** the whole milk into a saucepan and **add** cinnamon sticks. Turn the burner under the pan on medium.

2. Watch the milk carefully. When it's hot and steamy but not yet boiling, turn off the burner. (Do not allow the milk to boil.) Use a slotted spoon to **remove** the cinnamon sticks from the hot milk.

3. **Add** baking chocolate and chocolate chips to the milk. **Stir** with a wooden spoon until fully melted.

**4.** **Add** sugar and vanilla extract to the chocolate milk. **Stir** thoroughly with a whisk.

**5.** If needed, turn the burner on low to reheat for a few minutes. Then **ladle** the hot chocolate into mugs. **Garnish** each mug with ¼ cup mini marshmallows.

## TRY THIS!

To make peppermint hot chocolate, replace cinnamon sticks with one large candy cane and use ¼ teaspoon peppermint extract in addition to the vanilla extract. Garnish mugs with mini candy canes.

To make white hot chocolate, replace baking chocolate with white baking chocolate and the chocolate chips with white chocolate chips.

# Honey-Cinnamon Steamer

Here's a delicious way to warm up on a cold winter day.

serves 4

preparation time: 15 minutes

**ingredients:**

2½ cups whole milk
¼ cup honey
6 cinnamon sticks
¼ teaspoon ground cardamom
1 teaspoon vanilla extract

**equipment:**

liquid measuring cup
medium saucepan
measuring cup—¼ cup
measuring spoons
wooden spoon
whisk
4 mugs

1. **Pour** the whole milk into a saucepan. **Add** honey, cinnamon sticks, and cardamom, and **stir** with a wooden spoon to mix. Then turn the burner under the saucepan on medium.

2. Watch the milk carefully. When it's hot and steamy but not yet boiling, turn off the burner. (Do not allow the milk to boil.)

3. **Remove** the cinnamon sticks with a slotted spoon. **Add** vanilla extract, and stir with a whisk.

4. If needed, turn the burner on low to reheat for a few minutes. Then **ladle** into mugs to serve. **Garnish** each cup with one of the cinnamon sticks.

## SPECIAL INGREDIENTS

**allspice:** a ground spice made from dried allspice berries. Allspice is located in the spice aisle of most grocery stores.

**apple cider:** juice made from pressed apples. Unlike apple juice, apple cider is usually unprocessed and unfiltered. It can be found in the produce section of most grocery stores.

**baking chocolate:** a special chocolate that melts into a nice, creamy consistency when heated. High-quality semisweet baking chocolate contains 70 percent cacao. Baking chocolate can be found in the baking section of most grocery stores.

**cardamom:** an Indian spice made from the small seeds that grow inside cardamom pods. It can be found in the spices section of most grocery stores.

**cinnamon sticks:** natural spice sticks that add cinnamon flavor to drinks and dishes but are not eaten. They can be found in the spice section of most grocery stores.

**light coconut milk:** the creamy liquid inside coconuts. Light coconut milk is less thick and contains less fat than regular coconut milk. Canned coconut milk is available in the Asian food section of the grocery store.

**mango:** a tropical fruit with red, yellow, and green skin; a large pit; and sweet, bright orange flesh. Look for mangoes in the produce section of your local grocery store. If fresh mangoes are not available, frozen mango pieces may be available in the freezer section.

**maraschino cherries:** sweet, canned cherries, available in jars. They can be found near drink fixings or ice-cream toppings in your local grocery store.

**mint:** an herb used to flavor a variety of drinks and dishes. You can find fresh mint leaves in the produce section of most grocery stores.

## FURTHER READING AND WEBSITES

**Choose My Plate**
http://www.choosemyplate.gov
/children-over-five.html
Download coloring pages, play an interactive computer game, and get lots of nutrition information at this U.S. Department of Agriculture website.

**Cleary, Brian P.** *Food Is CATegorical* **series.** Minneapolis: Millbrook Press, 2011. This seven-book illustrated series offers a fun introduction to the food groups and other important health information.

**Farmers Markets Search**
http://apps.ams.usda.gov/FarmersMarkets/
Visit this site to find a farmers' market near you!

**Nissenberg, Sandra.** *The Everything Kids' Cookbook: From Mac 'n Cheese to Double Chocolate Chip Cookies — 90 Recipes to Have Some Finger-Lickin' Fun.* Avon, MA: Adams Media, 2008.
This cookbook is a great source for recipes kids love to make, including many drink ideas.

**Recipes**
http://www.sproutonline.com
/crafts-andrecipes/recipes
Find more fun and easy recipes for kids at this site.

## INDEX

# You're the Chef
# Metric Conversions

## VOLUME

| | |
|---|---|
| ⅛ teaspoon | 0.62 milliliters |
| ¼ teaspoon | 1.2 milliliters |
| ½ teaspoon | 2.5 milliliters |
| ¾ teaspoon | 3.7 milliliters |
| 1 teaspoon | 5 milliliters |
| ½ tablespoon | 7.4 milliliters |
| 1 tablespoon | 15 milliliters |
| ⅛ cup | 30 milliliters |
| ¼ cup | 59 milliliters |
| ⅓ cup | 79 milliliters |
| ½ cup | 118 milliliters |
| ⅔ cup | 158 milliliters |
| ¾ cup | 177 milliliters |
| 1 cup | 237 milliliters |
| 2 quarts (8 cups) | 1,893 milliliters |
| 3 fluid ounces | 89 milliliters |
| 12 fluid ounces | 355 milliliters |
| 24 fluid ounces | 710 milliliters |

## MASS (weight)

| | |
|---|---|
| 1 ounce | 28 grams |
| 3.4 ounces | 96 grams |
| 3.5 ounces | 99 grams |
| 4 ounces | 113 grams |
| 7 ounces | 198 grams |
| 8 ounces | 227 grams |
| 12 ounces | 340 grams |
| 14.5 ounces | 411 grams |
| 15 ounces | 425 grams |
| 15.25 ounces | 432 grams |
| 16 ounces (1 pound) | 454 grams |
| 17 ounces | 482 grams |
| 21 ounces | 595 grams |

## TEMPERATURE

| Fahrenheit | Celsius |
|---|---|
| 170° | 77° |
| 185° | 85° |
| 250° | 121° |
| 325° | 163° |
| 350° | 177° |
| 375° | 191° |
| 400° | 204° |
| 425° | 218° |
| 450° | 232° |

## LENGTH

| | |
|---|---|
| ¼ inch | 0.6 centimeters |
| ½ inch | 1.27 centimeters |
| 1 inch | 2.5 centimeters |
| 2 inches | 5 centimeters |
| 3 inches | 7.6 centimeters |
| 5 inches | 13 centimeters |
| 8 inches | 20 centimeters |
| 9 x 11 inches | 23 x 28 centimeters |
| 9 x 13 inches | 23 x 33 centimeters |